INTERNATIONAL CHRISTIAN
GRADUATE UNIVERSITY

THE HIDDEN RICHES OF SECRET PLACES

THE HIDDEN RICHES OF SECRET PLACES

Hazel McAlister

Thomas Nelson Publishers / Nashville

All rights reserved under International and Pan-American Conventions. Published in Nashville, Tennessee, by Thomas Nelson Inc., Publishers and simultaneously in Don Mills, Ontario, by Thomas Nelson & Sons (Canada) Limited. Manufactured in the United States of America.

Library of Congress Cataloging in Publication Data

McAlister, Hazel.
  The hidden riches of secret places.

  1. Meditations. I. Title.
BV4832.2.M14   242   79-25132
ISBN 0-8407-5718-2

To Helen Leonard
Louis Price
Shirley Johnson
Mary Tageliere

who   prodded
encouraged
reassured
and prayed—much.

To my family, for their inspiration, goes my deepest gratitude.

God
and
I
love
you
all.

I am a prisoner in chains,
walking to the guardhouse
of my very own prison,
yet wishing,
    longing,
     praying
to be free.

INTRODUCTION

"I being in the way, the Lord led me."
So said the servant of Abraham when he met Rebekah.
And I being in the way have too been led
through the wilderness—into green and pleasant meadows.
He led me in ways I could not understand
away from my comfortable, familiar paths
>—onto paths I didn't want to walk
>—to places I didn't want to go
>—to a church I didn't want to attend
>—to a Shepherd I didn't want to follow
>—into truths I didn't want to receive.

He led me in a new and better way.
>He chastised and loved me.
>He corrected and carried me.
>He reproved and understood me.
>He caused me to weep, and He dried my tears.
>He rejected my sin but did not reject me.

He showed me I was nothing.
He made me look at myself
>—when I was repulsed by what I saw.

He showed me Himself
>—and what I could be in Him.

He pushed and pressed and squeezed.
He drove me into difficult places
>—and when the burden was too heavy
>He bent down and carried it for me.

When my fainting heart caused my steps to fail,

He picked me up and carried me.
When my eyes spilled tears,
when my hands were bloody and torn
and the pain of hanging on was more than I could bear,
    He tenderly, carefully, and with great love
    washed the blood and stain away.
    He bathed me in the cleansing, cooling rain of heaven
    to comfort me.
He said, "Believe.
        Believe in Me.
        I will never leave you.
As you follow Me
I will change you, mold you, and make you
into the person
I long for you to be."
"Be," He said.
"Be. I want you to be like Me.
Behold. Believe. Become.
I want you to be like Me."
I knew His words, but I am learning how He thinks.
I knew His acts, but He is teaching me His ways.
I knew much about Him—now I'm learning to know Him.

What you will read here
are the things He is teaching me,
all learned on my walk to being who He wants me to be.
I have been compelled to share my thoughts and feelings
at the risk of being misunderstood.

I write in the firm conviction
that everyone hurts,
that we are all lonely,
that we hide,
that we all have secret places.
To write has taken all the courage He has given,
all the obedience I have learned.
And the greatest lesson I have learned is LOVE.

FOREWORD

Soon after returning from a trip to China, Hazel made a simple—but for her unusual—statement to her husband, Jack: "I have something I want to say. . . ."

Jack arranged for an interview with a journalist, which in the end did not bear fruit and after which he spoke these words of prognostication: "If you have something to say, I guess you're going to have to write it yourself."

She has . . . **The Hidden Riches of Secret Places** is the result.

My introduction to Hazel came in a prayer group two years ago. Pain and adversity were not written on her countenance but hidden somewhere far behind the smiling face. Compassion and a deep perception of the world of the spirit were also there. I could not have known then that Hazel McAlister was to become a warm and cherished friend.

Many people feel that because one is part of a family of prominence, through which a great, worldwide ministry flows, there must be a corresponding easy acquaintance with God. Hazel's poems and meditations dispel this wrongful view forever as the layers are unfolded to reveal that same agonizing groping after the Almighty that the rest of us experience at some time or another in our lives.

As she began to write what "she had to say," her mask began to slip and she grew fearful of what people would say about a Hazel McAlister unmasked, a Hazel McAlister letting it all hang out, a Hazel McAlister who was not the "all-together" person they had imagined.

But somehow the victory of the consecrated life seems so much more glorious when the Adversary has thrown all his forces against an individual and failed. Easy victory may come for some, and thank God for it; but for Hazel it has not been so.

To look on as another grows in humanity, as a stranger or friend experiences personal struggle and discovery, is only a part of this book. The rest is a matter of exploring the terrain of the spirit in which there are "rocks and hills and desperate valleys" and, with Hazel, becoming more and better along the way, finding "something of beauty" and "something of hope."

I had read no further than the introduction when I felt a sense of growing excitement. **The Hidden Riches of Secret Places** has the potential to change the way you live and relate to those around you, to challenge and even alter old attitudes, and to heal the wounds of the past.

As you close this book after reading it in one sitting or after choosing and reading an essay at random, I believe you will have been stimulated to a fresh quality of love and candor in sharing with the others in your life. That is more than exciting! For if all of us who are followers of Jesus could respond in this way, the revolution of love unleashed and the depth of forgiveness given could not only transform our families, our churches, and our institutions but could ultimately heal our nation, our planet, and all humankind.

Lory Patrick-Jones
(Mrs. Dean Jones)

IT WILL BE BEAUTIFUL

Wandering in the wilderness, the pathless, trackless wilderness,
is safe—
      lonely . . .
            desolate . . .
                  but safe—
and the territory is familiar.
The road to the Promised Land is not known to me;
it's untrod, untried, though close enough to me.
I cannot bear the pain of moving on.
I fear to go—I cannot stay.
What to do? Oh God, I wish I knew.
I face so many walls and confront so many giants,
I sometimes wonder if I can bear the pain.
Are the grapes worth what they will cost me?
What to do? Oh God, I wish I knew.
Such a wish expresses an anguished heart,
that though it sees no more
      and feels no more
            knows He is there.
I am learning the fellowship of His sufferings,
and He is creating something that He says will be beautiful.
Out of this wilderness land, what will He use?
Out of this desolate land, is there something of beauty?
Out of the rocks and hills and the quiet, desperate valleys,
      is there something of hope?
My helplessness shall be molded by His hand into something beautiful.

THE JOY OF THE LORD

Lynda bubbled; her eyes danced;
joy filled her heart and spilled out,
    infecting everyone she met.
She bounced over, threw her arms around me, and then happily exclaimed,
                        "I'm going to a saving.
                        I'm going to a saving."
I asked, "You are going where? What is a saving?"
Her face shone as she replied,
                "I'm going to tell my friends about Jesus,
                    and when I tell them how wonderful He is
                    and all of the good things He does,
                    I know they will want Him and be saved."
Full of excitement, she left to tell her longtime friends
about her new Friend, Jesus—the Giver of joy.
I stood there happy for her,
    but feeling a little sad and sorry for myself.
It had been a long time since I had experienced exuberant joy.
I prayed David's prayer from Psalm 51:12:
    "Restore unto me the joy of thy salvation . . . ."
I watched Lynda, a baby believer, who was just beginning
    her walk with Jesus,
almost fly down the street as she ran off to tell her friends
about her wonderful Jesus.
I prayed that she would never lose the unabashed joy she was feeling.
Joy because Jesus had
    touched her life,

washed her clean,
  forgiven her,
    and promised a bright, shining future.
Such joy—indescribable and reflecting itself in everyday life—
warmed and comforted me.
Trust,
  peace,
    confidence,
      are the constant companions of joy.

Prayers are prayed with assurance and expectancy where there is joy.
Joy lives easily and full in a clean,
      uncluttered,
      forgiving,
      tender heart.
Joy reigns abundant in the "right spirit."
Joy is one of the benefits of obedience—
 the greater the obedience, the greater the joy.
Joy is produced by Love (God is love, remember).
If you need more joy, you need more love (more of God, that's right).
Joy comes in direct relationship to love.
 Get your love relationships with Jesus
 and with others the way they should be,
and you will have great joy.
Be open,
  be transparent,
    touch others.
Allow them to touch you.
Give love, and joy will follow.

When you have no love of your own,
     give His love. It is perfect.
We experience joy by acquisition.
It is an exciting,
     pleasurable feeling
     that comes from keeping
     His commandments.
Love produces joy.
Jesus said in John 13:34,
     "A new commandment I give unto you, That ye love one another;
     as I have loved you, that ye also love one another."
In John 15:10,11 He said,
     "If ye keep my commandments, ye shall abide in my love; even as I have
     kept my Father's commandments, and abide in His love.
     These things have I spoken unto you, that my joy might remain in you,
     and that your joy might be full."
                         His love produces His joy.
It has been several years since Lynda went "to a saving."
Her friend is thriving in his walk with the Lord.
She still bubbles and continues to radiate
deep,
   settled,
     maturing,
        abiding joy.
Abide in My love, the Master said,
     and your joy will be full.

GOD'S SILENCE

Many of us uncomfortably suspect
that almost everyone has a better prayer life than we do.
We recognize the importance of prayer.
We know it is directly commanded.
    "Pray without ceasing," the Bible says.
We feel guilty about prayer and periodically resolve to develop
  a consistent, meaningful prayer life.
But somehow the good intentions are lost in the
    insistent, persistent demands of daily life.
Prayer is neglected, getting only little attention now and then.
Some of us think of prayer as a duty, something we need to do
  in order to walk with the Lord.
Some of us pray only in extreme emergency.
To some of us prayer is awkward, difficult, embarrassing.
To some prayer is abstract and without meaning.
But some people have found the secret of prayer.
They would never forget
    or neglect prayer.
They know that prayer is the right, the privilege, of every child of the King.
Prayer is the key
    to fulfillment,
        to happiness,
            and to a blessed life.
Prayer is a matchless opportunity
  to change people, problems, and situations.

To some prayer is a one-way street.
We do the talking.
We say many things—
things that have very little bearing on our everyday lives
    and our everyday needs. Then we say amen!

And God is silent.

In Bible days He spoke directly to men—
men like Solomon, Moses, Elijah, Daniel,
    and David, a man after His own heart.
It is not so today. We do not hear His voice.
God is often silent.
God's silence was deafening at Gethsemane.
Jesus the Son confronted the Father.
"Let this cup pass from Me," He prayed.

God was silent.

Jesus prayed, "Father, I will do Your will."

Still—silence.

Then Jesus prayed, "I will drink this cup; Thy will be done."
Again the Father answered with His silence.

Why is God silent today with us?
Do we dump our thoughts, our wrong requests, our selfish motives,
and our empty words on Him
    and then say
        amen?
My prayer life is sometimes like that.

I would not be able to hear His answer—and so God is silent.
He sends no guidance,
         no power,
         no refreshment,
         no answers,
Only silence.
Sometimes we go to God in anger,
   only to be chastened and comforted.
Sometimes we go to Him in confusion,
   only to be guided and enlightened.
But we must go to Him with worship, to praise and give thanks.
God's silence requires us to think and not to neglect our prayers.
Do not think He is silent because He doesn't care,
      or because He isn't listening.
God's silence speaks to our need to pause
   and to think about important things—
to learn of His grace, to find a turning point.
Don't neglect His silence. It could be His answer.
Hear Him speak
      His love—as for you alone
      His concern—for your smallest care
      His provision—for all of your needs
Hear Him in His silence.

The Son prayed—the silence filled Gethsemane—
"Father, if this cup may not pass away from Me
except I drink it, Thy will be done."
The Father answered His Son through His silence,
   and Jesus went to Calvary.

ANGRY AT GOD

He can be trusted;
He cannot fail.
>His nature decrees it,
>His word declares it,
>His love displays it.
Our God reigns,
and He cannot fail.

I was not yet fifteen, but
my heart felt as if it were being torn from my body.
My mind could not comprehend the words said to me.
My whole being screamed, "No, no, no.
>It can't be;
>>I won't believe it.
God wouldn't do that to me
>>or to my mother
>>or to my brothers.
How could He do that? It's not true.
My father is not dead."
My parents went to Pontiac to preach at a convention.
They left four days ago.
This is their twentieth wedding anniversary.
Daddy said he would be back in time to celebrate my birthday.
He told me he would be home, and he will be.
He went to the doctor before he accepted this preaching assignment
  and was told to forget that he had a heart problem.

He was well . . . The doctor was wrong . . . My father died.
While still on the platform after preaching the opening service,
   he had a heart attack.
The following afternoon at 1:15 he died.
At that same time I arrived home from school for lunch
and one of my father's friends was standing on our sunporch,
waiting to tell me that my father had had a heart attack.
It was a few hours later that we learned he had died.
I don't remember saying any of the things I was thinking
or feeling that day.
      The fear,
            the hurt,
                  the awful loneliness
                        are etched in my memory.
I will never forget the next day.
Our mother arrived home alone, brokenhearted,
   without her husband, our father.
The sound of her voice as she said, "I'm all alone," still rings in my ears.
Our friends came to love us and share our sorrow.
They sympathized, consoled, and tried to comfort us.
They prayed for us; they prayed with us.
None of them knew that this girl was angry and very, very frightened—
frightened because her adored and adoring father was gone
and angry at the God who had caused it
or who at least could have prevented it.
To be angry at God was inconceivable to me. I was terrified.
How could anyone dare to be angry with God?
I well remember telling God that if He could do that to me,
I wouldn't ever be able to trust Him.

Instead of giving Him my hand in humble submission,
I gave Him a clenched fist and a rebellious spirit that said,
"God, I will walk with You.
      I will serve You—but
      in a way that pleases me.
      You have caused me great hurt—therefore,
      You cannot have all of me."
Then I buried my anger.
It was buried so deep that eventually I forgot about it.
I didn't even know it was there.
Someone said,
"We bury our feelings and they grow."
Silently,
    stealthily,
        completely unknown to me,
           my anger grew.
It colored everything I thought—especially spiritual things.
It governed many of the things I did and caused me
  to make most of my mistakes.
I now know that to be angry is to be disobedient.
The natural outgrowth of disobedience is rebellion,
  and with rebellion comes an unclean heart, a wrong spirit,
      and ultimately more anger.
My anger could have destroyed me.
I'm human—
I'm like you are and suffer from the same things you do.
I want you to know and understand that I, too, am a person—
a rather ordinary lady who feels and reacts to situations as you do.
It is my prayer that you will realize that God can be trusted.

He will not fail.
>His nature decrees it.
>His word declares it.
>His love displays it.

Our God reigns, and He cannot fail.
He cares about me—even when I think no one else does.
He understands me—even when I don't understand myself—
and He loves me—as unlovely as I am
>with my anger,
>my mistakes,
>with all my failings.

He loves me. But He will not indulge me.
He loved me enough to stop me, to turn me around,
 and to lead me to a person who had
>the discernment to see,
>the courage to confront,
>and the love to listen while I talked.

I discovered that talking brings healing.
I had not talked—really talked—about me
>to anyone—ever.

It was difficult to do, more difficult than could be imagined.
But it was part of God's plan for me.
Someone had to point out
>the feelings that caused my emotional hurt,
>the thoughts that wounded my ego,
>the attitudes fostered by unlovely, subtle pride,
>and the anger that I had buried deep inside of me.

As those things surfaced, I was able to verbalize them to God.
Even though God knows everything, we must talk to Him

about the things that bother us in our hearts,
and as we converse and communicate with Him,
we free Him to forgive our anger,
           our resentment,
           our bitterness,
           our self-imposed guilt,
           our attitudes,
           and our actions.
They are all changed by the blood of His Son.
God allows different experiences to come into our lives
    to discipline us, to mold us,
        to make us, and shape us
           into His likeness.
Life is not always what we want or expect.
Life has its disappointments and hurts.
There is little we can do about much of it.
But how we respond to the things that life hands out,
    to the difficult things that God allows to come into our lives
is our responsibility.
To respond with anger,
        resentment,
        and a rebellious spirit
brings more problems to us and saddens His heart.
I am learning to respond with confidence in His ability to lead
and with trust in His love, knowing that He is in absolute control
and that there is always something to be thankful for.
Our bruised hearts will be healed; our anger will be dispelled—
    we can live in the glow of undisturbed peace and bring joy to His heart.

BE STILL

Be still and know.
If you wait for My timing
and listen to My voice,
you will stop hurting
and you will hear Me say,
 "I am God."

Be still and know that I am God.
Where did that voice come from?
Again in my heart the words,
Be still and know that I am God.
But I kept frantically, feverishly working,
  sorting,
   cleaning,
    arranging,
     rearranging,
busy doing nothing of any importance, endeavoring to forget yesterday's pain
and hoping to quiet the tumult in my heart and mind.

Our seventeen-year-old son, Gordon, was facing his fourth serious operation
for a tumor that grew in the inaccessible areas of his head
dangerously close to his brain.
These surgeries were very long,
    extremely difficult,
    hazardous to his life,
    bloodier than anyone could imagine,
    excruciatingly painful.

The surgeons worked with many problems.
The tumors were visible only by using mirrors.
The tentacles spread like spidery fingers,
   pushing bone and tissue out of their way
and in some instances fastening themselves to the skull.
The doctors worked with great care and much difficulty
trying to remove every tiny cell of the **angio fibroma**
that made my son's breathing almost impossible.
In the last twenty-two months we had already gone through
three of these operations.

I knew exactly what to expect
      —the pre-dawn drive to the hospital on the day of surgery.
      —the unbelievable hush as I sat at his bedside waiting and watching for
         the preoperative medication to take effect.
      —the furious beating of my heart when the orderlies carefully placed him
         on the hospital cot.
      —the love that anguished as we walked beside him down the long hall
         toward the swinging doors with the red sign that read
         NO ADMITTANCE EXCEPT TO AUTHORIZED PERSONNEL.
      —the final squeeze of the hand, the kiss and the whispered, "Son, you
         are loved—God will be with you."
      —The doors closing in front of us
         and the tears beginning to flow.

I didn't want to remember these things or the awful, interminable waiting,
waiting until the doctors would come to tell us the tumor had been removed.
Finally we would be allowed to peek into the recovery room
to see for ourselves that our son was still alive.

And then would come the days
    that often seemed to have no beginning or ending.
The pain would come—Gordon's pain—excruciating and unbearable,
and it would continue day after day.
Sitting, watching the agony of our son was almost more than I could endure.
Feeling that God Himself was totally indifferent,
                                    I ran.

From the minute the family left home in the morning
until just before they were due back again,
                                    I ran.

I tried to leave far behind me the pain I carried in my heart
and the cold hard lump that was in my stomach.
I shopped.
I visited friends.
I cleaned cupboards,
            closets,
            drawers,
            the house,
until there was nothing else to clean.
I tried desperately to ignore the questions that pounded in my head.
The Lord tried to minister His peace to me; but I kept running,
only to discover it was impossible to forget such painful memories.
I learned about the heavy heart
a mother carries for her child—
even a little of how God must have anguished for His Son.
There were times when I knew
I was learning to know Him by sharing His suffering.
He kept His promises;

He bore my pain and carried my burden.
He did that on those days I remembered "to be still and know that He is God."
(They were far too few in number.)

On this particular day, "being still" was far from my experience
or understanding. I was anything but still.
In my heart I knew that our son
was again just a few days away from much suffering,
perhaps even death.
On one of the earlier occasions our doctor had said of our son,
"He went so far down into the valley that only God brought him back."
I suppose I was afraid that God could not be trusted
to do the same thing one more time.
I had to learn over and over again
that our God can be counted on to do what is best for us.

> (Have you ever noticed in your own life
> how often you learn the same thing over and over again?)

I heard it repeatedly, "Be still and know that I am God . . . This situation is
out of your hands; there is nothing you can do—just be still. Don't try to do
anything. You can and you will know that I am God.
Quit your striving—it isn't necessary.
> Quit your running—you can't run far enough.
> Stop your murmurings—stop your questioning.
I will not leave you comfortless; you will know that I am God."
We did see God in that situation and in the many circumstances that have
come into our lives since that time. His word to us remains the same
> "Be still and know."

I am learning with difficulty that God is God. His ways are different. The only way to hear His gentle voice, to feel the nudging of His spirit, is to be still,

very still,

until He carves into our hearts
three simple words,
"He is God."

The boy is now a man who knows the Lord.
Most of his time is spent counselling—helping others.
Gordon is caring,
gentle,
strong.
The man who was once a boy
is married to slender, intelligent, pretty Elisabeth.
We enjoy a love relationship.
Gordon and Elisabeth,
my son, my daughter,
and my very good friends.

CHARLIE BROWN HELPS

"Sometimes I feel as significant as a bug."
Lucy said those words to Charlie Brown.
They were a good description of the way I felt.
Nothing was working out right.
It appeared that God and man had purposed to thwart
   every good desire in my life.
I was having the "blahs," and I didn't like the things going on inside of me.
I was sitting around in my faded three-year-old robe,
drinking cold coffee and reading the newspaper.
My house was in a shambles, and I didn't want to clean it.
The laundry was piled high—the washing machine was broken,
      and I did not want to go to the laundromat.
I hurt, I really hurt.
My husband was too rushed to find out why I was so perturbed.
In fact, he left in a huff; I don't think he even said goodbye.
God was so far away;
I was afraid He had forgotten me and didn't know where I lived.
But—God never goes away.
    He cannot forget us, and
        He always knows where we live;
and so I decided to read the Bible—but that didn't help.
I tried Oswald Chamber's **My Utmost for His Highest**—that didn't help.
I went to **God Calling** (author unknown) and that didn't help.
Then I went to Charlie Brown in the morning newspaper—
        Charlie Brown helped.
I couldn't believe what God used to cut through the fog.
Lucy and Charlie Brown—

I would never have believed they would bring the Word of the Lord to me.
"Sometimes I feel as significant as a bug."
Now that is the truth.
Here I sit in my messy house with my unwashed face and uncombed hair,
feeling like a bug and praying no one will knock on the door.
A bug—what a perfect picture of me.
The mental picture I drew from that cartoon made me laugh.
It pulled me out of my lethargy long enough to know that
someone understood—even if it was only Lucy.

By coincidence—
   not really coincidence for that is not possible in our walk with the Lord—
I began to think about the woman in Mark 5.
She is mentioned in only a few verses—a woman without a name.
For all of my life she has been to me a woman without a face.
All I ever saw in those verses of Scripture
was a woman who was ill for twelve years—
a woman with enough faith to push her way through a crowd
and touch the hem of Christ's robe.
Today I see a woman wearing my face—wearing your face—
a woman whose name should be "All Women Everywhere."
Come with me back almost two thousand years,
to the defeated country of Israel, into the area of Galilee.
Put on the loose-flowing robe, wear the sandals of that day,
and walk with the woman who is wearing your face.
She could be someone in her late twenties, or in her thirties.
She and her husband probably have four or five children.
They live in a small, poorly-cared-for home.
She has been menstruating continuously for twelve years.

Think about her condition.
Physically she is anemic.
The medical care is at best limited,
the sanitation almost nonexistent.
She hardly has enough physical strength to get through the day.
Her house is probably a mess,
She doesn't have the energy to do her work—
        it must no doubt be done by her children.
        We all know how that works out; at best it's not very good.

Let's talk about her husband—or maybe we'd rather not.
How would your husband react if you had been sick for twelve years?
I know how my husband would act.
He'd try to be kind and understanding, but he's busy—pushed and pulled.
                It would be tough.
Because it would be difficult for him, it would be more trying for me.
Imagine the financial condition of this family.
In a conquered country, money is scarce.
After going to one doctor after another for twelve years, plus all the extra
expense that illness brings, you can imagine the mess they are in.

Think about the emotional state of this woman who wears our face.
She is emotionally spent and exhausted,
        financially deprived,
        a physical disaster.
Her home is in a state of disrepair;
        her family is in an uproar.
She is living in quiet desperation,
        not knowing where to go for help.
feeling as significant as a bug.

And then—someone tells her about Jesus.
Hope begins to stir in her heart.
Her mind can hardly conceive the wonderful things
she hears about this amazing Man.
She knows she must find Him.
But in her weakened physical condition, how can she?
Where is He, this Man who performs miracles?
If she finds Him, how can she approach Him?
She is ashamed—
    ashamed of her disease,
        embarrassed by her history,
            dismayed by her total image.
The desire to find Him, just to see Him,
is so intense she ignores all the difficulties.
Forgetting how fearful she is and how inadequate she feels,
she sets out in tearful desperation to find Jesus.
She is too bashful to come to Him boldly,
as the others come to plead their causes.
I think she is afraid of what her neighbors will say.
They know her condition.
She might even be intimidated by Jesus, panicky about taking His time,
in all probability thinking she does not deserve
to be close to this incredible Man.

This insignificant woman with our face—our name—
slips unnoticed through the crowd,
only to fall on her knees and touch the border of His robe.
She must be trembling from head to foot as He turns and says,
"Who touched Me?"

"Lord," the disciples say, "everyone is touching You. How can you ask 'Who touched Me?' "
He only smiles as He replies,
"Faith touched me. I was not jostled by the crowd. This touch was purposeful, pleading, hopeful.
Virtue flowed out of Me. Where is the one who touched Me?"

Picture in your imagination
the surprise of neighbors and friends as this woman who wears our face says,
"Lord, it was I. I touched You."
And then picture the love and the gratitude that flood her face
as Jesus says, "Woman, your faith has made you whole."
I believe that means physically,
    financially,
        spiritually,
            emotionally
                WHOLE.
All because this woman who wears our face reached out and touched Him.

This morning Lucy reached out and touched me.
She caused me to remember Jesus, my Lord,
the One who is concerned about all things, even insignificant bugs.
I was like that woman—
choked by the dust,
    lost in the crowd,
        desperate for change.
Despite the insignificance I felt, I reached out, grabbed, and held onto Jesus,
and He made me whole.

FOUR LETTER WORDS

Obey is a four-letter word.
> I don't like four-letter words.

Must obey,
> again, four-letter words.
> I don't like four-letter words.

Can't obey.
Won't obey.
> More four-letter words.

I must obey.
I will obey.
Submission,
that's love.
Love is a four-letter word.
> I like four-letter words.

Let me tell you about my friend, Nancy,
> friendly, smiling, pretty Nancy, with
one of the sweetest faces you have ever seen.
Few people would ever know
that behind those smiling brown eyes
was once a resentful, bitter spirit.
Not always bitter, and not toward everyone—
> certainly not toward me, her good friend,
> > nor toward her children.
But she was bitter toward her husband—some of the time,
> her pastor—much of the time,
> > her church—almost all of the time.

One day during a telephone conversation
Nancy was relating an experience of
"submission," as she called it,
submission to her husband,
a good-looking, spiritually oriented, professional man,
a man with a vital commitment
       to his Lord,
            to his family,
                  and to his church.
Of course, he has his faults, but who doesn't?
But Nancy, like so many of us, concentrated on them.
On this particular day it was with gritted teeth and set jaw that
she rather grimly said, "At least I submitted."
                        My heart almost stopped beating.
I knew I had to say something to my dear friend,
       something that would hurt,
            that would cause her to cry,
                  something she could misunderstand.
It could even cost a friendship that I treasured.
I had heard the same words I was about to speak.
I knew they would hurt, and so
with all the love and gentleness I could muster, I managed to say,
       "No, Nancy, you are not submitting . . .
            you are merely obeying."

There was dead silence on the other end of the line.
I don't remember how or when the conversation ended,
       or even if it had an ending.
I only know I had wounded a friend.

I later learned that on Nancy's calendar that day was marked
"the day Hazel attacked me."

God is love—and God is good.
    He knew my heart and my motives.
    He knew her heart and her motives.
And the words that I was prompted to speak on that day
    took courage and great risk,
but they bore fruit—much fruit.
Nancy learned the difference
    between the words
    obey and **submit.**
The truth of Proverbs 27:6 became reality to each of us:
    "Faithful are the wounds of a friend."
First comes obedience—it's so difficult to learn.
Most of us learn through suffering.
Then we learn submission,
    a much finer form of obedience.
            Obedience is an act of the will.
        Submission becomes an attitude of the heart.

Nancy was laughing as she said,
"Obey really is a four-letter word,
    and I don't like it."
I had asked what good things had happened
since our conversation on the subject of obedience and submission.
She was still laughing as she continued,
"You mean that shocking, hard-to-hear truth?"
"Yes, dear friend, that's what I mean," I answered.
She became serious as she replied.

"I cried for three days,
but when I really looked at myself and thought about my attitudes,
I was shocked, because I knew that what you had said was true.
I was not submissive, and if I wanted to mature spiritually
I had to change—in my heart.
It was necessary to stop obeying;
I didn't like the idea of obedience—
          in fact I resented having to do it.
I asked the Lord to teach me what He wanted me to know about submission.
It hasn't been easy to learn.
Old habit patterns are hard to break;
      thought patterns are difficult to change—
          but He is helping me,
and submission becomes easier as I practice it.
I am happier.
      My husband is happier.
          My children are more relaxed.
I have given up my desire (unconscious to be sure)
    to be the head of this family.
My husband has his right place as priest in this home
as I continue to trust him and his plans.
He is more accepting of me and my ideas.
My life as a wife and mother becomes more and more together.
The children are unconsciously aware that good things are happening to us.
Therefore good things are happening to them.
I almost never feel resentful; our new church is wonderful.
So many of the impossible situations are becoming possible.
The little things, the big things, all are falling into the right places.
So many of the things that were important to me no longer are.

My desires are changing; I enjoy doing the things that please my husband.
Yesterday I even enjoyed mowing the lawn.
I hate to sound super-spiritual,
but I thanked the Lord for a sharp lawn mower."

We both laughed.
We knew Nancy had learned submission.
Submission is an attitude of the heart.

INTERNATIONAL CHRISTIAN
GRADUATE UNIVERSITY

PEACE IS A GIFT

The noise was unbelievable,
the place was in an uproar,
as parents, grandparents,
relatives, and friends
rudely jostled and crowded one another
trying to press their faces against the window
for a better look at the newborn babies
who were housed in the
understaffed nursery
of the neighborhood hospital.
It was feeding
     and changing time.
Tiny arms and fists flailed the air,
as the screaming, outraged babies
          protested against the misery
          of wet diapers and empty stomachs.
We watched with concerned amusement
as the nurses
took them one at a time
out of the tiny beds they were lying in
and handled them with casual
     but loving care.
Quickly
and skillfully they changed the wet diapers
and dressed the red, wrinkled little bodies
of tomorrow's protesters.

My attention was drawn to a crib
that was cradling a relaxed,
                    sleeping,
                    peaceful baby—
a baby smaller than the others,
        warmed by the light of an incubator,
                fed automatically by intravenous feeding,
a baby completely unaware
        of all of the noise and confusion,
                sound asleep in the middle of turmoil.

What a picture of peace.
Surrounded but not touched.
Encompassed but not dismayed.
Protected,
            warmed,
                nourished,
peace in the middle of turmoil.
Webster says:
        "Peace is freedom from war or strife, an undisturbed state of mind,
        absence of mental conflict, serenity, calm, quiet, tranquility."
Peace not dependent on circumstance.
Peace in the eye of a hurricane.
Peace on bright,
        sunlit days,
Peace in the shadows,
        in the happy times,
        and in the sad times.

Constant,
continuing,
undisturbed,
indestructible,
peace is
    a gift from God.
People the world over
        long for it,
           cry for it,
              even die for it.

It is ours—
His gift to us
as we walk with Him
through the varied circumstances
of abundant living.

JESUS NEVER CHANGES – REALLY?

I was surprised and somewhat puzzled
as I sat one bright spring morning in a sunlit chapel.
I was to be the speaker for a women's fellowship meeting.
Just before going into the meeting,
the organization president asked me
to begin my talk with a personal testimony.
I wondered what could be said in three minutes
that would make sense and be of benefit
to the ladies that were present that morning.
Frustrated, I was sitting—waiting
for the business and the preliminaries to be over.
Suddenly the words I had been looking at—
words carved from wood,
decoratively set on the chapel wall—
came alive.
They were words that bring life;
they blazed at me as though illuminated by some unknown source.
"Jesus Christ the same yesterday, and to day, and for ever" (Heb. 13:8).
Surprise and puzzlement
came with my careful examination of the meaning of those words.
Jesus Christ the same? I thought. **That's not true.**
He has changed.
    He is different.
        He is more real to me.
            He is my true Friend.
                He is always with me.
                    He even talks to me, and that is different.

But, I mused, **those words are truth.**
Hebrews 13:8 is Scripture, and all Scripture is truth.
It is God's Word to us and cannot change.
I wondered how I could possibly feel that those words,
known to me all of my life, were not true.
My unbelief was not the arrogant unbelief of the agnostic
nor the skepticism of the cynic—
it was honest questioning that filled me with amazement,
because I really do know that what the Bible says is true.

Gradually I realized that God was trying to say something to me.
He wanted to tell me that He is the same.
He has never changed, but I have changed.
He is remolding and remodeling me.
The quality of my life is changed by the quality of His blood.
I wondered if that were possible.
Has the inferior quality of my life changed
because of the superior quality of His blood?
Yes, it has.
I cannot explain how.
I only know that the superior quality of His blood
is continually being applied to
        my thoughts,
        my attitudes,
        my talk,
        and my ideals.
They are all being changed.
His blood gives life and banishes death,
        covers the blots and the marks
        that sin has made on our bodies.

Jesus' blood has changed my life.
In Him and by Him I possess everything I need
to live a life of superior quality.
Jesus' living His life in and through me is changing me,
and in that process I've learned to know Him
in a new and different way.
Once I knew Him only as the majestic Lord,
the Creator and Ruler of the universe.
But today I know Him also as my loving Friend and Guide.

He is the Lord who has wept with me and tenderly dried my tears.
He is visibly moved with compassion.
He hurts because I hurt.
He binds up my wounds and heals my bruises.
When I am betrayed and rejected, He holds me close
and whispers that He, too, has been betrayed and rejected
and knows the pain I feel.
He understands my weaknesses
and in their place gives me His strength.
He gives me hope when all hope disappears.
He causes my desert places to become green.
He makes the rough places smooth,
and turns the mountains into beautiful hills
that are not difficult to climb.

No, this amazing Man has not changed.
But I have.
I have learned to know Him better and love Him more.

ETERNAL POSSESSIONS

The helicopter with its searchlight brighter than day
was flying overhead, blaring out the words,
"Evacuate, evacuate."
We were awakened from a sound sleep at two o'clock in the morning.
The police were banging on the front door.
Our neighbors were already in the street,
calling to those of us who had not yet left our homes.
Our feet hit the floor.
My husband raised the window shade to reveal
a sky red with fire.
Smoke filled our nostrils.
The unfinished building next door was enveloped in flames.
The helicopter, still roaring overhead,
made another pass over our condominium,
this time barely clearing the housetop.
We were able to understand much more clearly.
"Evacuate immediately. Gasoline explosion expected. Evacuate. Evacuate."
"Hurry. Put on your robe and slippers.
They must be afraid the garages will catch fire—if that happens . . .
Just hurry. Don't do anything unnecessary.
We have to get out of here."
My husband continued, "I'll put Buffy on her leash, and we'll get out of here."
Buffy was the gorgeous, blond, brown-eyed canine member of our family.
During the two or three minutes since we had been awakened, Buffy had
cowered at the end of the bed, sensing that something was wrong.
At the mention of her name and the word "leash,"
she jumped off of the bed, wagging her tail.

She knew she would go for a walk and a run in the park.
Her eyes were calm, her fear gone;
her master was in control.
We didn't even bother to lock the door
  as we left our little townhouse condominium.
We knew that in a few minutes
the whole place could be in ashes.
I realized there had not been time to take my purse—
    the family pictures—
        my father's watch—
            not even the important papers—
                or any of the so-called valuables that we
                    all plan to take if it is necessary
                    to hurriedly leave our homes.
My husband, Buffy, and I walked out to the street,
and with our neighbors we watched as the flames
grew higher and closer to the rows of attached garages,
most of them housing two automobiles.
It would take one spark in the right place and approximately
eighty cars and forty-three homes would go up in a popcorn-type explosion.
In a few minutes everything could be gone,
and forty-three families would be destitute.
As we watched, waited, and wondered I could hardly believe
that a routine evening had taken such a startling turn.
I don't remember much about what we said or thought that night
while we stood in nightclothes on the sidewalk.
I only know that we did not feel the panic
or the distressed confusion
our neighbors appeared to be feeling.

It was strange and unusual to know that all
of our personal and material possessions could be gone
in a matter of a few minutes.
We have lovely things—things given to us by people
who have been in almost every corner of the world,
beautiful, distinctive-looking things that I enjoy.
There were lovely things that had belonged to my mother
        —thoughtful gifts given to us by our children, purchased with the dimes
           and quarters they had lovingly and carefully saved.
        —things from small children that say "Mom and Dad, we love you."
These things are irreplaceable—
the accumulation of thirty years of married living.
I really didn't want to lose them.

It was two hours before the fire was out,
and then it was safe for us to return to our homes.
We said goodnight to our neighbors,
and in a few minutes we were back in bed,
contented and enjoying the sleep that comes from knowing God.
I learned the next morning that our neighbors had gathered
in one of the homes,
too upset and excited to sleep.
They had spent the rest of the night worrying and dreading the next day,
wondering where we had gone and not being able to imagine
that anyone could have been relaxed enough
to fall asleep.
I longed for them to know His peace.
A few days later my dear friend Helen said,
"Hazel, what would you have done and how would you have felt if

you had lost all of those beautiful things you have in your home?
Some of them are collector's items.
Would you have tried to replace them?"
My immediate response was,
"No. Those things are no longer important to me.
I would not have replaced them.
As lovely as they are,
they still are only things—
possessions.
I possess them.
They don't possess me."
(Until that moment I was not sure of that.)
"We would have replaced the necessary things,
but the extras—the lovely things—no."

My answer gave me tremendous satisfaction.
I knew my priorities were right,
pleasing to Him and to me.
I had lived a long time before finding out how unimportant **"things" are.**
My treasures are incorruptible,
              lasting and durable,
              precious and valuable.
Their value is beyond calculation.
They are indestructible
when the fire comes or sudden tragedy strikes,
things we are so apt to take for granted—
    like friendship,
        love, peace,
           a sense of well-being,

contentment of spirit,
joy of forgiving,
freedom of forgiveness,
and many more things that cannot be destroyed.
I am indeed blessed and grateful.

FROM ORDINARY TO SPECTACULAR

One day while flying over the Canadian Rocky Mountains
I was filled with awe and wonderment at their majestic grandeur.
The beauty of God's handiwork was overwhelming.
Those mountains are unbelievable in their splendor.
From the depths of my being
I worshiped the God who had created them.
From the deep recesses of my heart I cried,
        "Lord, I would like to be that spectacular
        to You, but I am such a nothing."
Immediately and without hesitation the words of Genesis 1:2
flashed into my mind.
      "And the earth was without form, and void;
       and darkness was upon the face of the deep.
       And the Spirit of God moved upon the face of the waters."
What a picture of me—especially on that day—
in the dark, without form, a void.
I knew better than anyone else that I was as powerless
as this old earth to make myself into something beautiful.
But a God who could from nothing
create a world that was sensational
could surely take a person like me,
created in His image,
and make her into someone spectacular,
    if she were willing to
      submit to His
        molding,
          fashioning,

carving,
        and fitting her
                into His design.

My heart became a battleground.
My spirit cringed.
I thought about
giving up my ideas,
                dreams,
                and desires,
letting go of the things I treasured
and placing myself totally,
        absolutely,
                and finally into His hands,
to allow the Holy Spirit free reign in my life.
I thought about the tears,
        the tearing,
                and the wounding
required for my submission.
The battle raged, and I exhausted myself.
The decision was mine, only mine.
No one else could make it for me.
I knew submission requires an act of the will,
and if I wanted to be "spectacular to God"
I must "will"
to submit.

Leaving the exquisite creation of the Rockies,
we flew over the foothills of the same mountain range,
        drab, ordinary little hills.

In a sudden burst of understanding
I knew why the Rockies
were so much more beautiful than these hills—
    the valleys were deeper,
        the hills were steeper,
            the peaks were rockier,
                the crags were craggier,
                    and the glaciers were almost inaccessible.
God's carving,
        cutting,
                splitting,
                    and chiseling—
minutely detailed—
had fashioned the Rockies with great care.
The result was the difference between
ordinary and spectacular.

Could God,
        would God,
take me—a nothing—an ordinary lady—
and create something spectacular?
    He could,
        if I would
            submit.

BOUND TO A POWDER KEG

Hope and faith.
You may be afraid to hope,
but hope you must.
Faith is the substance of things
hoped for;
therefore if I have faith,
or if I'm going to have faith,
I must hope.

When you feel as though you are bound and leashed
to a keg of powder,
fearing that it will explode and blow
    you,
        your world,
            and everything in it
into a thousand minuscule pieces,
that is the time to have faith.
If all of your faith
gets up and runs away,
then
have hope.
Hope against hope, the apostle Paul says.
Hope—
it is the glue of faith.

When the pressures of living
    have exhausted you,

and all of your dreams lie shattered,
and everything within you
feels despair;
when all you can do is hope
and pray
that the keg of powder to which you are bound
will explode,
because your present world is
unbearable the way it is;
when it seems that a thousand little pieces of anything
are better than the pain
of being
bound to a keg of powder,
that is the time you must have hope
and the courage to have faith.
Lean on the Lord.
If you know Him, act as though you do.
Don't be confused by your own ability to reason.
Be confident;
respond quickly—do the things He would have you do.
Trust the little things that
He is continually doing.
Allow the Holy Spirit to have His way in you.
Respond obediently to the things He teaches you.
Know that He is not dependent on your actions;
realize that you are
totally
and utterly
dependent on Him.

He will cause your hope to become faith,
faith that He will keep you moving
in the right direction.
He **is** in control of the powder
in the keg to which you are bound and leashed.

NEVER ALONE

If you feel as though you are in a quagmire
and nobody cares about you,
that you can't count on anything
      —or anyone—
and you are not even sure
    Jesus knows who you are
    or where you live or even if He cares,
Remember: He does know,
        He does care—
        His Word says so.
"Lo, I am with you alway, even unto the end of the world" (Matt. 28:20).
"I will never leave thee nor forsake thee" (Heb. 13:5).
Those are the words of Jesus.
He is touched
    by every feeling of our weakness.
In every trying circumstance
    He is there.

Not very long ago I found myself feeling completely alone,
thinking that no one really cared.
I decided to go on a trip.
I was trusting God to show me He cared.
My husband was busy evangelizing the world, and
he had almost lost sight of me.
He knew I was a fairly independent, self-contained lady.
I would be all right,
and his busyness wasn't too much of a problem to me.
I should be able to understand.

I did understand.

He was too busy for me.

And I wasn't all that important, anyway.

I didn't like it.

My response was such that he allowed himself
to become more involved in his work
and was at home less and less.

Our daughter was having a rough time.

I was hurting for her.

Our son and daughter-in-law had just resigned
an associate pastor's
position.

I was hurting for them.

Feeling that everyone who was important to me
was in some kind of a distressing situation,
I would not let them know I was downhearted and discouraged.

The truth is, I was really too proud to say,

"Kids, this is your mother, and she hurts."

It is a fearful thing to find yourself in a position of leadership,
needing help yourself but afraid to reveal your heart.

The difficulty is in finding
someone trustworthy enough to be comfortable with,
someone with whom you can be transparent.

I am grateful God has since given me
a few people who care, who will allow transparency.

But at that time the people I thought cared had betrayed my trust.

I was really alone.

The solution was to get away and find out for myself
—by myself—
if God could be counted on.

I confess to you that in my loneliness and hurt
I was doubtful and fearful
He might just let me wander on and on and on.
But **God does care.**
He revealed Himself in such simplicity
I will never forget His special tenderness to me
       —one of His suffering children.

My lovely little copper-colored Ford Torino
was glistening in the sun as I went roaring down a country road.
The solitude and sense of freedom settling on me felt good.
No one in my family
or any of my friends
knew exactly where I was
     or when I was to arrive at my intended destination.
I was revelling in the quiet—when
a loud noise jarred me from my hypnotic quiet.
My car swerved out of control.
I was frightened . . .
     until an unseen Presence took control of my car and
     guided it to the side of the road.

The tires on my automobile were new;
the blowout should never have happened.
A few seconds earlier I had been enjoying going nowhere in particular
in the peace of a deserted area on a lonely country road.
Now this.
I got out of my car.
Seeing my ruined tire alarmed me.

Here I was, all by myself,
    in a bleak, forsaken area
        —no one knew exactly where I was.
There had not been another car
in sight for more than an hour.
What on earth was I to do?
My situation seemed desperate.
I could be gone for days before anyone would miss me.
Then in the distance I saw a rapidly approaching car.
Out there by myself in this desolate place,
I had a few moments of panic.
Who was in the car that was hurtling toward me,
and what would they do when they saw me?
The little red sports car slowed as it came close.
I prayed a fast prayer for protection.
Almost before the car had come to a complete stop,
a young man jumped out on the passenger's side.
"Lady," he said, "Are you in trouble?"
"Yes, as a matter of fact. I don't know how to change a tire."
He was joined by the driver of the car.
"That's okay, lady. We'll help. Let us change your tire."
"That would be great. I didn't know what I was going to do.
Thank you very much."
My tire was changed in about ten minutes,
during which time these fine young men gave me a short lecture
on driving in deserted areas without knowing how to change a tire.
Then they advised me
to take a safer route,
one on which I could find a store to buy a new tire.

Somewhat chagrined,
I thanked them for their help.
They waved goodbye, got back into their car,
    and barrelled on down the road.
I turned my car around
and took the safer route.

My heart was stirred and touched
as I began to think of the providence of God.
My heart was saying,
"Lord, thank You.
No one
    —not one person—
        knew where I was.
Thank You for sending those young men to help."
So sweetly He whispered,
"I knew where you were.
I will always know where you are.
And when
you are in trouble,
I will send someone along
to turn you in the direction you should go."
He knows where we are,
        even if we don't.
The truth I have known in my mind
        became experience.
He does care.
My eyes burned with tears of joy.
I am not alone.

DON'T PANIC

I had a full-blown case of hysterics.
The feelings that engulfed me will never be forgotten.
It all began when my husband called from our home in California.
"I've just had a delightful Father's Day."
>How could this possibly be?
>I was visiting in eastern Canada.
>We lived in southern California.
>Our children lived in northern California.
"Lorilyn [our twenty-two-year-old daughter] surprised me with a visit," he continued.
>"How lovely—I'm delighted.
>How is she?
>How did she come?
>Why did she come when she knew I was away?
>Is she all right?"
>The questions tumbled out of my mouth.
"Lorilyn brought Peter home to meet me," he said.
>"Oh, no," I replied.
"Have you ever met Peter?" he asked.
>I barely managed to whisper, "Yes, several times."
>After my heart resumed its normal beating, I asked,
>"Is she going to marry Peter?"
"She will tell you about it when you get home."
I was three thousand miles from home, in another country.
Lorilyn hadn't lived at home for two years.
She came home while I was away
—something she had never done before.

Her father wouldn't tell me why.

My mind ran rampant.

I allowed myself to become more upset and agitated by the minute.

> "Is she getting married?
> Is she already married?
> Did you like Peter?
> I had hoped she would go back to school.
> Is Peter working?
> How is it with Peter and the Lord?
> Lorilyn and Peter are so different.
> How could she possibly think about marrying him?
> What in the world is she thinking about?
> Their backgrounds . . . can't she see. . . ."

"Now, darling, slow down," my husband gently cautioned me.

"Remember what Paul said, 'Cast down imaginations.'

Be calm and talk with her when you get home.

You will be completely satisfied with the things she will tell you."

He said goodbye and hung up.

He was satisfied.

I wasn't—not if she were going to be married.

She's not ready for marriage.

She needs to continue her education.

Peter isn't ready for marriage—he's immature.

He doesn't have it together.

On and on my imagination raced.

How will he ever support her?

She will have to work all her life.

She needs to become an R.N.—that's what she wants and needs.

"Cast down imaginations," the Holy Spirit whispered in my heart.

"O.K., Lord. This kind of destructive thinking
could drive me insane.
If You will help me, I will quit fretting about it."
This was more than fretting.
My mind and emotions were in a state of hysteria,
while I appeared perfectly cool and calm on the outside,
a lady who really had it together.

How many other people react in that way,
looking and acting as though they didn't have a care in the world?
Just below the surface they are basket cases,
feeling as if their whole world is falling apart.
Their emotions are like smashed eggshells.

In my heart I knew I was guilty of that kind of behavior
more often than I cared to admit
—guilty of not showing my true feelings,
     of smiling,
             of always acting as if everything were all right.
If I had problems, I certainly didn't want anyone else to know about them.
It was necessary for me to be in control
of myself and of my emotions at all times,
to show that I could handle the things
that hurt and bruised and caused me to cry.
The realization of the personal dishonesty
of that behavior was distasteful to me.
It was time to work on that neglected area of my life.
Not that I wanted to fall apart, have hysterics, or scream and cry—
I just wanted to narrow the gap between the outside and the inside
and allow the Holy Spirit to mold my emotional nature,

to change the imaginations of my mind
to resemble the calm and cool exterior
I was able to maintain on almost any occasion.
And thus began a work that is continuing to this day.
    It's trying;
        it hurts;
            it's not easy.
It's extremely difficult being remolded into His image.
The Scripture clearly says I possess His mind.
Beyond any doubt the words in 2 Timothy 1:7 are true:
"God hath not given us the spirit of fear;
but of power, and of love, and of a sound mind."
I'm delighted that as the days pass
it is easier to cast down the imaginations of my mind
and allow His peace to fill my heart.
The Lord works His will
when we get our heart and our heads where He wants them to be
            —in His hands.
I turned the whole "thing" over to Him
            —Lorilyn, Peter, wedding, me—
all of it.
As gently as He could,
the Holy Spirit reminded me of the time a few months before
when I had again committed my darling daughter to Him and said,
"Lord, she is Yours,
    her life,
        her future,
            her career,
                her talent is all Yours.

She was Yours before she was ours; You love her.
I can't plan her life; You already have the plan
         —and have had it since the beginning of time.
Please, Lord, You work it out as You see fit.
I'll take my hands off.
She is Yours—all Yours."
I did take my hands off.
It wasn't easy, but He helped me.
He had never stopped working from the minute she was born,
and He will not stop until the day she stands before Him.
She is His child—the child of His love.
He is going to take good care of His special creation.

After arriving home I discovered they did have wedding plans.
I was terrified, but we planned a wedding.
Lorilyn was going to wear the gown
I had worn at my own wedding so many years before.
It would have been a lovely wedding.
The reception would have been charming.
But as we planned and prepared, we prayed.
God continued His work in her.
As He revealed His plan for Lorilyn's life
she came to know that His plan did not include marriage to Peter.

Less than four weeks before the wedding,
      the dresses were ready,
            the invitations addressed,
                  the reception plans finally completed.
There was nothing to do but the last-minute details
and then the celebration—but for what?

Our daughter was marrying the wrong man.
The ringing of the phone interrupted my thoughts.
My heart was heavy as I answered it.
"Hi, Mom." It was Lorilyn.
Her voice was quiet.
She sounded sad.
I knew immediately that she was troubled.
"Honey, what's wrong? Has something happened?"
My happy little bride had become a subdued, somber young lady.
"Mom, I'm not sure about Peter.
I don't know what to do.
I'm frightened.
When I get married it will be for life.
I don't know if I want to spend the rest of my life married to Peter
. . . but I love him.
What can I do? . . .
Her voice trailed off as she continued, "I don't seem to feel sure."
I said, "If there is even a little doubt in your mind,
wait—be sure.
This wedding doesn't have to take place now.
Take plenty of time; think it over carefully.
It isn't necessary to decide now.
You have until eight o'clock September 3 to finally make up your mind."
"Mom, could you handle that?"
"Yes, I could handle it even if you walked half way down the aisle
and still changed your mind.
This is your life we are talking about.
Nothing is as important as that."
"What would we tell the people?

They would think I'm just a dumb kid who doesn't know her own mind."
"Honey, we wouldn't tell the people anything.
Dad would take care of that."
She giggled when she thought about how well
    her father could handle that situation.
"Actually, Lorilyn, Dad and everyone else will be pleased
that you have the inner strength to re-examine your feelings.
That takes courage.
Don't decide now; wait a few days."
We talked some more and placed it all in God's hands.
And again He showed me how much He could be trusted
if I allowed Him to work.
The secret is
"allowing"
Him to work.
After hanging up the phone,
I thanked God for giving me the wisdom to keep my mouth shut
so that Lorilyn could hear His voice more clearly.
In just three more days she came home to tell us
that she had postponed the wedding.
Lorilyn is back home going to college,
pursuing a career in nursing,
and following the God that loved her too much to let her
make a mistake.
This mother's heart rejoices and is grateful to God
for this special care and love He is bestowing on her daughter.
God is good.
He can be trusted to do His work, in His way, in His time.
But we must take our hands off and let Him.

HOME SHAPERS

When you are tired and bored and feeling useless
because all you do is
>the cleaning,
>>the shopping,
>>>the dishes,
>>>>the laundry,
and all of the other everyday things we mothers do,
think about the things
—the good and important things—
our families are learning from us.

We were delighted and happy when
our daughter moved back home.
One day, not long ago, I was preparing dinner.
It had been a dark, rainy day, and now it was
dusk—the best time of day.
The kitchen was fragrant with the smell of homemade soup
and of a custard baking slowly in the oven.
The table was set; everything was ready
for my family who would soon be home.
I was filled with peace and well-being
knowing they would be pleased
with the dinner I had just prepared.
I knew also that it was becoming easier to learn
some of the lovely things
the Father was trying to teach me
—not realizing that in a few minutes

He would teach me another
    unforgettable,
        attitude-changing
            truth.
Our daughter was the instrument He used.
Lorilyn walked into the kitchen,
put her arms around me, and said,
"Mom, when I saw my clean and folded clothes on my bed,
I realized how much I could count on your love.
My clothes are ready even before I need them. You do so many things for me.
I don't even have to think about them.
You are always there.
But Mother, that's not all.
I know I can depend on your love, and
you are helping me understand God's
    constant,
        consistent,
            unfailing love."
And we get bored and restless "just"
        being homemakers.
We are not homemakers;
we are home-shapers
and miracle-workers.
David Ben Gurion said,
    "An Israeli is a realist
    who believes in miracles."
A Christian wife or mother
    should be a realist
    who believes in miracles,

Not only in the big ones—
      the turning of water into wine,
      the crossing of the Red Sea—
but a realist who believes in
everyday miracles,
the ones that go by unnoticed or even unrecognized
as miracles.
Miracles like the breaking of a new day,
the song of the baby bird as he leaves the nest in his first freedom flight,
or the youngster who faces each day
    with the vitality,
      anticipation,
        and excitement
   that only the very young enjoy.
Or the miracle that happens when your child throws his arms
around your legs and squeals,
"Mommy, I love you—you are the best mommy anybody ever had,"
(even though this has been one of your grouchy mornings).
Or the miracle that happens early in the day
   when your husband looks at you,
     in your worn-out robe
       with your hair uncombed
         and the look of sleep still on your face
  and says with love and tenderness,
    "Honey, you're beautiful,"
and you know you're not,
but in his eyes you are.
          That's a miracle
           of love.

WALLS

Behind the wall I stand
    alone,
        sad,
            reflective,
                weighed down,
hugging my hurts and disappointments to me
(they provide a strange security),
unguarded from the darts of the evil one,
unprotected from the imaginings of my mind . . .
    from the past erupting around me . . .
        from the future looming in the shadows.

Outside the wall I stand
    with Him,
        contented,
            unblemished,
                confident in His accepting love,
guarded by the fidelity of His constant presence,
protected by the tenacity of the Holy Spirit.
The past, behind me, is forgiven;
the future is unknown, outside my control;
but I'm secure because of Him.

Even though I am afraid
to venture out from behind my wall,
I must take the risk
and expose my fragile feelings

in the vulnerability
of close, honest relationships.
Venturing out from behind my wall causes me
to re-think, re-sort, and review
the feelings of being used and abused
and the tearful, hurting defeat
of the last time I emerged.
Hundreds of unanswered questions pound in my head.
But I know that to build a wall to keep hurt out
always keeps hurt in.
To venture out
requires me to
trust
His love
and His ability to understand
my constant, earnest desire
for an open,
honest relationship
with Him,
      my family,
          and my friends.
When we refuse to be vulnerable
and limit what we say to each other,
ultimately we have nothing to say
and relationships cease.
To risk vulnerability with open,
honest conversation
and loving confrontation
brings healing to our angry thoughts,

           our confused ideas,
                and our bewildering emotions,
                     and, finally, restores the spirit.
To air our disappointments in such a way as
to accuse a friend of rejection and of causing pain
is to blame another for our actions.
This blocks future communication,
brings guilt and condemnation,
and prevents
the open, honest relationships
that our hearts long for.
However—
to avoid confrontation
is to perpetuate conflict
and destructive anger.
We must take responsibility for the
pain and rejection we feel.
We must go to our friends (after heart-searching prayer)
and confront them (without placing blame),
with a loving, caring attitude
           and a right spirit,
saying, "I have reacted to the things you said
and all that you have done
with unbalanced emotions that bring me pain
and cause bitter thoughts
that force me to feel sad and bereft.
It is my desire
to rid myself of the sting
from those destructive feelings."

Confronting this way
is to confront with love
          and without blame.
Such behavior and attitude of spirit
will open the heart
to be released
and healed.

Life brings many hurtful happenings and trying experiences.
How we react to them
can either enrich
or embitter us.
To respond with sensitivity and grace
will create the environment
that repairs broken hearts
and the fragmented
shattered relationships
of the desperate,
lost people
around us.
It is only as we have suffered
from our own lack of virtue,
known times of complete failure,
that we are able to
effectively refresh
and refill others.
It has been said
"Every meeting of persons is an exchange of gifts."
My prayer on meeting the

battered,
shattered people
of my world
is to reach out,
        touch,
        and give
the loving, understanding care
that has been given to me.
As we give compassionate understanding,
we are able to comprehend
the reasons that we walked
the deep,
        dark,
        desperate valleys.
Those trying, pain-filled days
and lonely, sleepless nights
have taught truths and ideals
that can minister life
to the death that surrounds us.

As we come out from behind our walls,
        relate to others,
                share our experiences,
                        make ourselves vulnerable,
we become useful and effective.
                        Lord,
                help me to be a caring,
                        conscientious,
                administrator of Your life.

FREE TO FAIL

Today I blew it,
and I feel as if I have been
    hit by a truck,
        run over by a tractor,
            and dragged by a horse
all at the same time.
This has been one of those
nightmarish days
that we hear about
        and read about
        and pray we will never have.
I feel as though all of life
and every demon in hell
have conspired
to make this day horrendous.
Nothing has worked out right.
I am being engulfed.
The day is drowning me.
Some days it is easy
to trust
and to love.
This is not one of those days;
it has been intolerable.
I feel as if God
has gone fishing,
and there is nothing I can do about it.
I have never felt such spiritual pain.

Does God care
      that this day feels
      like a bleeding wound?
My head tells me He does.
But my heart cries so loudly
it cannot hear my head.
If God cares—
and I know He does—
maybe He is only asleep.
But they say
God never sleeps.
Why then this hopeless feeling
and this helpless pain?
Nothing is working out right.
Everything I have tried to do
has failed.
Success is nowhere
to be found.
Failure.
Every place I turn
I am up against a wall.
            The car needs repair.
            The insurance is due.
            The dentist's bill is leering at me.
            There just isn't enough money to meet all the demands.
            The gas lines are two hours long.
            The cleaners lost a good dress.
            My doctor of twenty-five years is retiring in four weeks.

My hairdresser has been hospitalized.
We had an invasion of sow bugs
    (they're ugly little creatures).
My diet isn't working.
    I am starving myself
    and feeling deprived and
    my clothes don't fit,
    even my panty hose are tight.
I feel like a failure—
a great big,
    giant-sized
        failure.

Earlier today,
with a calm, quiet spirit,
I tried to right a wrong.
Who of us can right a wrong?
I failed at that.
No one seemed to understand
or even care
that I had
a hurting heart.
The phone has been ringing this whole trying day.
My friends are failing, too.
They were listening for the
logical thinking
and the practical ideas,
even intelligent advice,
that I am sometimes able to give.

But this is one of those days
when everything is flying apart,
and I have no counsel
or comfort for myself or my friends.
The refrigerator is empty,
and the cupboard shelves almost bare,
and I do not want to go to the market.
The house is filled and rocking
with the banging, clanging noise
of my neighbor's stereo.
I want to run away.
My head is pounding.
My blood pressure must be higher than the sky.
My nerves are screaming.
The tears are gushing down my face.
In complete frustration
I drop to my knees and cry
"Lord,
I really messed it up
I feel like a rat
caught in a trap,
        pushing,
               pulling,
                      struggling,
to be free.
Please, Lord, forgive me.
Free me from this trap.
I don't want to mess it all up
like I did today.

Lord, I come to You so often,
pleading for forgiveness.
Again
and again
I come to beg for Your forgiveness.
I've been so caught up
in the miseries of life that
I didn't spend enough time with You
today
or yesterday.
Please forgive me for today.
One more time, Lord,
I need to be forgiven.
> My attitudes are wrong,
> my thoughts so petty,
> my feelings so bitter,
> my desires so shallow.
Tomorrow will be better.
I will find success
from the failure of today."
I am almost hysterical when
I barely hear Him say,
"Again, my child?
You failed again?
I don't remember that you
ever failed before."

A FORGIVING SPIRIT

Forgiveness should be a life-style
and not a one-time event.
A forgiving spirit should be a desire of the heart.
The psalmist David, asking for forgiveness, prayed,
"Wash me thoroughly from mine iniquity" (Ps. 51:2).
Some of us have never progressed
beyond our initial meeting with Him
and have closed our eyes
    and our ears
to any teaching that concerns
going to the cross daily
for fresh forgiveness—
forgiveness unto righteousness
  and into the overflowing, abundant life
    that He has created us to enjoy.
To know that we can be forgiven
for the bad attitudes that rob,
    the feelings that steal,
      and the ideas that erode
any possibility of vital, vibrant relationships
is beyond our comprehension.
Not only is daily forgiveness possible,
it is absolutely necessary if we are to be victorious
in our walk with Him.
The need for forgiveness
    for each other,
      from each other,

and from Him
is paramount.
Forgiveness is one of the most beautiful
experiences of life,
both in the giving
and in the receiving.
God forgives and forgets.
He buries all of our sins
in a sea of forgetfulness.
When we forgive,
it is hard to forget.
But it is possible
if we allow
His forgiveness to overflow us.
A Christian leader has said
"When a person will not forgive another,
he prevents himself from enjoying the forgiveness of God.
It is not that God will not forgive,
but the unforgiving one is preoccupied with the
offense to himself
and is not receptive to God's mercy."
When we truly and completely forgive,
we are able to forget.
Perhaps not as totally as God forgets—
but the hurt,
    the sting,
    the bitter resentfulness
are all forgotten
as we allow His forgiveness to flow through us.

No, it is not easy to forgive.
But the rewards
to ourselves
and to the ones we have forgiven
are immeasurable
and as pure gold.

On one occasion
I knew I had to ask forgiveness,
not because of some overt action on my part,
but because of sinful thoughts and attitudes
that were like daggers in my heart.
I was being robbed
of every good thing
God wanted to do for me.
The reasons
for my attitudes were almost justifiable.
Anyone's attitude would have been the same.
No one would blame me.
          No one but God.
One day He put His finger on
a very hurtful area of my heart
and said, "I want to heal that hurt.
You are suffering unnecessarily.
My Son died so you would not
bear that agony.
Release it;
let it go."
I cried, "Lord, I don't know how. I can't."

His answer—"Apologize."
I screamed, "Lord, I haven't done anything.
You've got your wires crossed.
Let me tell You what she did to me.
Why should I apologize?"
His answer came loud and clear:

"Your attitude is like a stench in my nostrils.
            It is stifling your life.
            You are being robbed of my blessing.
What has been done to you
has no relationship to what
I am telling you to do.
Apologize."
"Lord, I don't want to."
Then, it was as though God closed a door on me.
There was to be no discussion,
        no rationalization,
            no compromising,
                no arguments on my behalf.
I was to do
what He had commanded.
We warred—not God and I—
but the me who wanted God's best and
the me who wanted my own desires,
            the me who was holding the hurt.
Fortunately, and with some aid from the Holy Spirit,
the me who wanted God's way won out.
There was no other way.

God would accept nothing else
        but absolute obedience
        and total surrender.

I made the necessary appointment
to begin what I expected to be an
act of full restoration,
ending in happiness ever after.
It didn't work out that way.
The appointment was broken
by a third person.
I was humiliated and dumbfounded.
What was the meaning of this?
In a few days I thought I saw the benefits of that event:
I wouldn't be embarrassed by a
face-to-face meeting.
Apology would not be necessary.
I wrapped myself in self-righteousness
and told God I had done what He had asked
        but it hadn't worked.
        It wasn't my fault.
        I had tried;
        therefore I would not apologize.
It is gross audacity to tell God
you tried to do His bidding,
        but it didn't work.
His very firm response was that I must try again
    and again
        and, if necessary, again

until His purpose was accomplished.
I rebelled.
Finally,
with much inward protesting
I made another phone call.
Would you believe she wasn't there?
I left my name (so she could call me).
She didn't,
and I begrudgingly made a
third phone call.
This time, apparent success.
The appointment was made
and kept.
The results? They were far less than satisfactory to me.
      I was listened to with cool politeness
      and very little verbal response.
Was I forgiven by the lady involved?
    Probably, but I am not really sure.
Did a long and lasting friendship emerge?
    No!
Are we able to engage in meaningful conversation now?
    No!
Do I still feel bitter and resentful?
    Almost never,
but when I do,
we (my feelings and I) go immediately to the cross
and say "Father, please forgive.
      I don't want to feel that way.
      Replace that spiteful feeling with your love.

I want my life to please You.
Cause Your forgiveness to flow through me,
reflect the life of your Son in me.
Thank you for forgiveness
and a richer,
fuller life."

I am learning that when God requires a specific
action from us,
the outcome is not our responsibility.
Our **only** responsibility is to do His bidding.
Forgiveness can never be a one-time event.
It must be a life-style.
A forgiving spirit is of maximum importance
—and must be earnestly sought.
It grows as we forgive.
As we are obedient and forgive, the Father will reveal His heart to us.
God Himself is the Supreme Forgiver.
As we forgive, the attributes of the Father's character become ours.
He has committed Himself to forgive us.
When we forgive—
not as man forgives but as God does—
We release ourselves
and others
into the manifold blessings of God.
Forgiving is truly one
of life's most God-like experiences.

LEFTOVERS

"Our relationship with God deserves more than leftover time."
I shall never forget the impact these words had on me.
They leaped out of the page I was reading,
and I read them again and again.
They burned like a hot iron
into my heart and brain.
I knew that in those words lay the reason
for so much of the loneliness
and the heartbreaking solitude of the
     useless,
         restless,
              searching years.
It was time left over from
     my husband,
     our children,
     cleaning the house,
     driving the carpool,
     doing the laundry,
     entertaining friends,
     running to the market
         and to the doctor
         and to the dentist—
     even time left over from attending church
     and working in women's groups
and from the myriad of things
     that we housewives are involved in
     —all of them good,

most of them necessary,
   but often done at the wrong time
   and in the wrong order.
All I had left to give to my relationship with Jesus was the time left over
from all these other activities.
In reality He deserved—and should have had—
       the first time,
           the best time,
               the quality time.
All of those other good things and people
should have had the leftover time.

He gave up
the glory and the splendor
of His Father's home.
He set aside
the majesty of His deity
and became a stranger
in a foreign land.
God became a Man
and took on Himself
the frailties of humanity.
He was a Man who was hungry,
       who became thirsty,
       who wept.
He was lonely,
       rejected,
       laughed at,
       mocked,

beaten,
and finally crucified.
He became sin
—not just like sin—
but
He literally became sin.
He who was the perfect, sinless
Son of God
took on Himself
every sin known to man.
He suffered hell
for me.
And all I gave Him
was the ragged
tag-ends
of my frantic days.
Small wonder that my days
often ran together in
harried,
hurried
nothingness.
I should have been giving Him
the best time of my day.

In the early morning
when our home was filled with a happy hush and
the family was still sleeping,
I would quietly slip out of the bedroom
to sit in the big green chair by the window.
I would savor my mug of steaming coffee

while
watching the dawn
    slowly,
        silently
            push away the darkness.
Then I would read the morning newspaper with leisure,
while the fire in the fireplace
thrust its lovely, laughing shadows
into the early morning peace.
My heart was warmed with the knowledge
that my sleeping family
would soon be up
and the hush would give way
to a hustling,
    bustling,
    busy day.
As I lovingly hoarded the memories
of these mornings,
I realized that He had wanted to be included.
He had desired quiet, intimate time with me
        before the day pressed in on me.
He longed for me to share His Word,
        worship Him,
        love Him,
        listen to His voice,
        feel the glow of His presence,
and sometimes just to be there,
His silent companion.
I knew I needed

all of those things
from Him.
But, oh, the wonder of knowing
He desired that
from me.

BE FREE

"Stand fast therefore in the liberty wherewith Christ hath made us free"
(Gal. 5:1).
"If the Son therefore shall make you free, ye shall be free indeed"
(John 8:36).
Those words are a part of my vocabulary.
They are a very real part of the heritage
given to me by my parents.
I had read them and read them.
I had heard them over and over again.
I had repeated them innumerable times over the years
    to myself,
       to my friends,
         to my children,
and many times to the countless classes I had taught.
But they were not a vital part of my life and understanding
until a few days ago.
I realized one unforgettable morning
I was in prison—
walking in chains
in my very own prison,
yet, wishing, longing, praying
to be free.
Suddenly my prison became intolerable to me.
I could no longer endure the guilt,
agony, loneliness, fears and frustrations.
All the bleeding from my sins
(forgiven, to be sure)

was too much for me to bear.
The guilt and condemnation were too heavy for me to carry.
The fear that family, friends, and associates would find out
the things I carried as bruises on my heart,
the scars on my soul from years past, became more than I could handle.
I should have walked away from this stinking, putrefying garbage.
The deeds committed in the flesh had long since
been forgiven and forgotten by Him.
But those same sins were destroying me.
      I had not forgotten them.
Satan used them as a club to rob me in every way possible,
of my abilities,
    my drives,
        even of my very life.
My energies for anything constructive were
    sapped,
    fragmented,
    dissipated,
    destroyed.
I had allowed myself to be imprisoned—
Not in His prison, but in my prison.
I had created it with the imaginings of my mind,
built it with fears that almost consumed me.
But the psalmist said, "He hath broken the gates of brass,
and cut the bars of iron in sunder" (Ps. 107:16).
The apostle Paul said, "There is therefore now no condemnation to them
which are in Christ Jesus" (Rom. 8:1).
Even though I had known those verses since I was a small child,
I didn't really know them at all.

Early one morning the truth of those words
crashed into my heart and pierced me to the innermost part of my soul.
"There is therefore now no condemnation to them which are in Christ Jesus,
who walk not after the flesh, but after the Spirit."
Are those words true—really true?
"The truth shall make you free" (John 8:32). I remembered that one, too.
Are those words true—can they bring life?
"Lord, are those Your words to bring life?
Do You really understand how I feel?
Do You really know about my prison?
Lord, how could You who did not sin
understand the wounds,
    the tearing,
        the scars of my sin?"
I heard the answer over and over in my heart.
"Sin is sin, my child. There are no shades of sin.
All people have sinned, and all sin demands the death penalty;
all were condemned to die.
I became sin for you.
I was tempted in all the same ways you are,
and because I yielded not and stood in your place
I bore the penalty of your sin so you can be free.
To Me, you are as though you have never sinned.
I have given you My nature, My goodness,
My life, My love,
My purity, My honor.
I have dressed you in My white robe of right-ness.
There is now no condemnation.
You are in Me, and I am in you.

You are free."
Suddenly the **now** no condemnation,
the **is** free took on new meaning.
I was released from my prison—
the prison of my guilty feelings
and my great fears—
free from ever again being bludgeoned with the heavy club of my past failures.
The Son has set me free and there is now **no** condemnation.
I need never again be afraid of what man
can or will do to me.
I am protected and kept by the blood of Jesus
and enveloped from head to toe in His robe.
I am free.

After engaging in countless conversations with people
who love and follow Jesus,
those who are absolutely sure
their sins are forgiven,
I am of the opinion that many,
if not all of us,
carry as wounds in our hearts
a heavy load of unnecessary, unwarranted guilt,
marring our lives and scarring our souls.
Each one of us is a unique,
unusual creation,
and the things that Satan hounds
and harasses us with
are different.
It would be unwise and inappropriate

to enumerate
the accumulation of things
that prick our hearts like thorns and bristles
or to note the things that continually plague us,
then leave us
bankrupt and broken.
Nor would I suggest that suddenly
some morning
you will awaken
illuminated
with a new understanding of the words
"There is now no condemnation."
God deals with each of us
as He knows us—
as individuals
with amazingly different personalities.
But I know,
without a hint of doubt,
that
His desire and plan for us
is that we walk
in freedom—
free
from the crushing attacks
of the one who would chip, tarnish, and diminish
the very essence of life.

     In Jesus' name,
      Be free.
      Live.

AN UNSUNG HERO

Today my brother* met his Master.
He looked into His face.
Imagine if you can
the joy
that filled his heart
when the Father looked at him,
smiled, and said,
"Son, you are without sin.
You stand before Me dressed in the
righteous robe of My other Son.
You have fought a good fight.
Your life in My presence will now begin."
Imagine if you can
the love that overwhelmed my brother
when he looked into the face,
held the hands,
and kissed the feet
of his Redeemer.
No, my brother is not dead.
He is more alive today than ever before.
He is worshiping the Father,
glorifying the Son,
and enjoying the beauty and majesty
of his new home forever.
Blessed be the name of the Lord.

*Gordon Swanson

My brother was a good man.
When he died and we buried him,
everybody came to say that he was a good man,
that they had loved him, and that they would miss him.
But the sad fact is, none of us knew
what a really good man he was.
And the sadder fact is, he didn't know how much we loved him.
And now that he has gone, we are all sad
because a good man lived with us
and a good man walked among us
and we really didn't know how good he was.
My brother could be counted on;
he carried us all in his heart
        and in his love.
His love was quiet
        and very deep.
My brother's love could be depended upon.
He remembered us all in his prayers:
    Carol, Debbie, Jim
    Mother, Jim, Hazel.
We were his family,
and we counted on his prayers.
My brother was a good man,
    brother of two,
    husband of one,
    father of two,
    uncle to several,
    pastor to some,
    friend to many.
My brother was a good man.

His son called him unique;
   our brother called him an uncommon man,
   and I called him brother and friend.
His friends said he was great.
They called him loyal and faithful,
   constant and devoted,
      unusual and dependable,
       caring and loving.
Many said he was special,
and all of us agreed.
We all gathered,
his heart-broken family and friends.
We sent flowers,
we talked,
we even laughed a little
as we remembered the funny things.
We knew we all would miss him,
and we held each other and cried
the day we honored my brother
after he had died.
Lord, please tell my brother
how much we really loved him,
how very much we miss him
now that he is home with You.

With tender voice the Lord replied,
"Not now. I'll wait.
We'll all tell him together
when you've come home, too."

THROUGH IT ALL

Through it all
Through it all
I've learned to trust in Jesus,
I've learned to trust in God.
Through it all
Through it all
I've learned to depend upon His Word.*

—ANDRAÉ CROUCH

      Through it all . . .
every agonizing minute,
every trying day,
in the gloom of lonely nights,
in the sunlight of the good times
       . . . I've learned . . .
So many things.
Good things, long ago forgotten,
have been re-learned,
new things added to those things already learned.
All of life is a learning process,
a time of acquiring knowledge.
I've learned through these past days
   demanding,
      exhausting,
         exciting days—
      . . . to trust . . .

Trust,
what a word that is.
Babies are born with it;
little children have it in abundance,
but we adults, perverse and disillusioned as we are,
must learn how to trust.
To trust is to have confidence in,
to know He is faithful
and will not fail us.
My thoughts go to the times God whispered,
"Do you trust Me?"
I would answer, "Lord, you know I trust You.
If I didn't, I wouldn't be here.
I wouldn't be taking on some of these difficult things."
I would go on and on,
selling the Lord on the reasons I trusted Him.
He knew, as I now know, that
trust needs no explanation.
Trust **is**—simply **is.**
He whispered again and again in my heart,
"Hazel, do you trust Me?"
With confidence I now answer,
"Yes, Lord, I trust You."
He knows I have learned to trust
        . . . in Jesus. . .
Jesus fills me with wonderment
because of His mighty, tender, humble dealings with me.
He is my Friend,
my incredible Friend.

Jesus.
He has conquered me,
and because of Him I am a conqueror.
I've learned to trust in God. . .
God,
the Father,
the Almighty,
all-merciful King of Kings,
the Creator God who watches over me,
God, the One who is worthy of worship.
I worship Him for who He is;
I praise Him for all of His goodness to me.
I thank Him for His Son Jesus.
I've learned to depend. . .
Depend—I love that word.
It's another word for **trust,**
to count on,
to have faith in,
to stand
. . .upon His Word*
This is the starting place,
the road map that points to final fulfillment.
I've learned to depend upon His Word,
His unchangeable Word.

*Quoted from the song "Through It All" by Andraé Crouch.
Copyright © 1971 by Manna Music, Inc., 2111 Kenmere Ave., Burbank, CA 91504.
International copyright secured. All rights reserved. Used by permission.